Landscape Consequences of Natural Gas Extraction in Lackawanna and Wayne Counties, Pennsylvania, 2004–2010

By L.E. Milheim, E.T. Slonecker, C.M. Roig-Silva, and A.R. Malizia

Open-File Report 2013–1227

U.S. Department of the Interior
U.S. Geological Survey

U.S. Department of the Interior
SALLY JEWELL, Secretary

U.S. Geological Survey
Suzette M. Kimball, Acting Director

U.S. Geological Survey, Reston, Virginia: 2013

For more information on the USGS—the Federal source for science about the Earth,
its natural and living resources, natural hazards, and the environment—visit
http://www.usgs.gov or call 1–888–ASK–USGS

For an overview of USGS information products, including maps, imagery, and publications, visit
http://www.usgs.gov/pubprod

To order this and other USGS information products, visit http://store.usgs.gov

Suggested citation:
Milheim, L.E., Slonecker, E.T., Roig-Silva, C.M., and Malizia, A.R., 2013, Landscape consequences of natural gas
extraction in Lackawanna and Wayne Counties, Pennsylvania, 2004–2010: U.S. Geological Survey Open-File
Report 2013–1227, 32 p., http://pubs.usgs.gov/of/2013/1227

Contents

Figures

Tables

Conversion Factors

Multiply	By	To obtain
Length		
mile (mi)	1.609	kilometer (km)
Area		
acre	4,047	square meter (m^2)
acre	0.4047	hectare (ha)

SI to Inch/Pound

Multiply	By	To obtain
Length		
meter (m)	3.281	foot (ft)
kilometer (km)	0.6214	mile (mi)
Area		
square meter (m^2)	0.0002471	acre
hectare (ha)	2.471	acre

Horizontal coordinate information is referenced to the North American Datum of 1983 (NAD 83).

Landscape Consequences of Natural Gas Extraction in Lackawanna and Wayne Counties, Pennsylvania, 2004–2010

By L.E. Milheim, E.T. Slonecker, C.M. Roig-Silva, and A.R. Malizia

Abstract

Increased demands for cleaner burning energy, coupled with the relatively recent technological advances in accessing unconventional hydrocarbon-rich geologic formations, have led to an intense effort to find and extract natural gas from various underground sources around the country. One of these sources, the Marcellus Shale, located in the Allegheny Plateau, is currently undergoing extensive drilling and production. The technology used to extract gas in the Marcellus Shale is known as hydraulic fracturing and has garnered much attention because of its use of large amounts of fresh water, its use of proprietary fluids for the hydraulic-fracturing process, its potential to release contaminants into the environment, and its potential effect on water resources. Nonetheless, development of natural gas extraction wells in the Marcellus Shale is only part of the overall natural gas story in this area of Pennsylvania. Conventional natural gas wells, which sometimes use the same technique, are commonly located in the same general area as the Marcellus Shale and are frequently developed in clusters across the landscape. The combined effects of these two natural gas extraction methods create potentially serious patterns of disturbance on the landscape. This document quantifies the landscape changes and consequences of natural gas extraction for Lackawanna County and Wayne County in Pennsylvania between 2004 and 2010. Patterns of landscape disturbance related to natural gas extraction activities were collected and digitized using National Agriculture Imagery Program (NAIP) imagery for 2004, 2005/2006, 2008, and 2010. The disturbance patterns were then used to measure changes in land cover and land use using the National Land Cover Database (NLCD) of 2001. A series of landscape metrics is also used to quantify these changes and is included in this publication.

Introduction: Natural Gas Extraction

The need for cleaner burning energy, coupled with the relatively recent technological advances in accessing hydrocarbon-rich geologic formations, has led to an intense effort to find and extract natural gas from various underground sources around the country. One of these formations, the Marcellus Shale, is currently the target of extensive drilling and production in the Allegheny Plateau. Marcellus Shale generally extends from New York to West Virginia as shown in figure 1 (Coleman and others, 2011). Coleman and others (2011) defined assessment units (AU) of Marcellus Shale production based on the geology of the region.

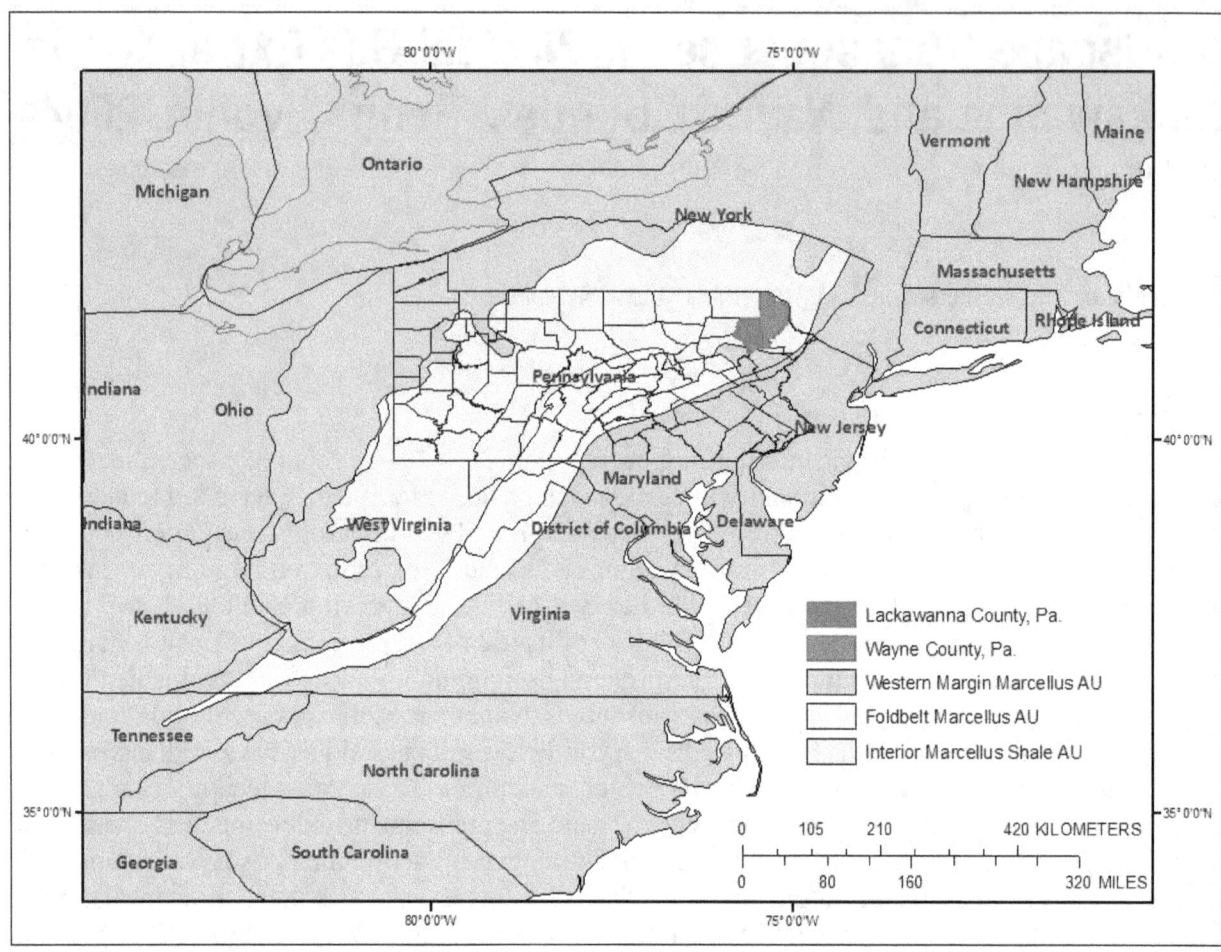

Figure 1. Map of the Appalachian Basin Province showing the three Marcellus Shale assessment units (AU), which encompass the extent of the Middle Devonian from its zero-isopach edge in the west to its erosional truncation within the Appalachian fold and thrust belt in the east. The Interior Marcellus Shale AU is expected to be a major production area for natural gas (Coleman and others, 2011). Base-map data courtesy of *The National Map* [(*http://viewer.nationalmap.gov/viewer*) (U.S. Geological Survey, 2011a)].

The overall landscape effects of natural gas development have been considerable. Over 9,600 Marcellus Shale gas drilling permits and over 49,500 non-Marcellus Shale permits have been issued from 2000 to 2011 in Pennsylvania (Pennsylvania Department of Environmental Protection, 2011) and over 2,300 Marcellus Shale permits in West Virginia (West Virginia Geological and Economic Survey, 2011), with most of the development activity occurring since 2005.

The Marcellus Shale is generally 600 to 3,000 meters (m) below the land surface (Coleman and others, 2011). Gas and petroleum liquids are produced with a combination of vertical and horizontal drilling techniques, coupled with a process of hydraulically fracturing the shale formation, known as "fracking," which releases the natural gas.

The hydraulic-fracturing process has garnered much attention because of its use of large amounts of fresh water, its use of proprietary fluids for the hydraulic-fracturing process, its potential to release contaminants into the environment, and its potential effect on groundwater and drinking-water resources.

Development of natural gas wells in the Marcellus Shale is only part of the overall natural gas story in this area. Conventional natural gas wells are commonly located in the same general area as the Marcellus Shale AU. Conventional wells generally are much shallower and less productive than Marcellus Shale wells and commonly are located in clusters that cover large areas of the landscape with nearly 60,000 total gas wells established. Both types of well may affect a given area. With the accompanying areas of disturbance, well pads, new roads, and pipelines from both types of natural gas wells, the effect on the landscape is often dramatic. Figure 2 shows a pattern of landscape change from forest to forest interspersed with gas extraction infrastructure. These landscape effects have consequences for the ecosystems, wildlife, and human populations that are collocated with natural gas extraction activities. This document examines the landscape consequences of gas extraction for two areas of current Marcellus Shale and non-Marcellus Shale natural gas extraction activity.

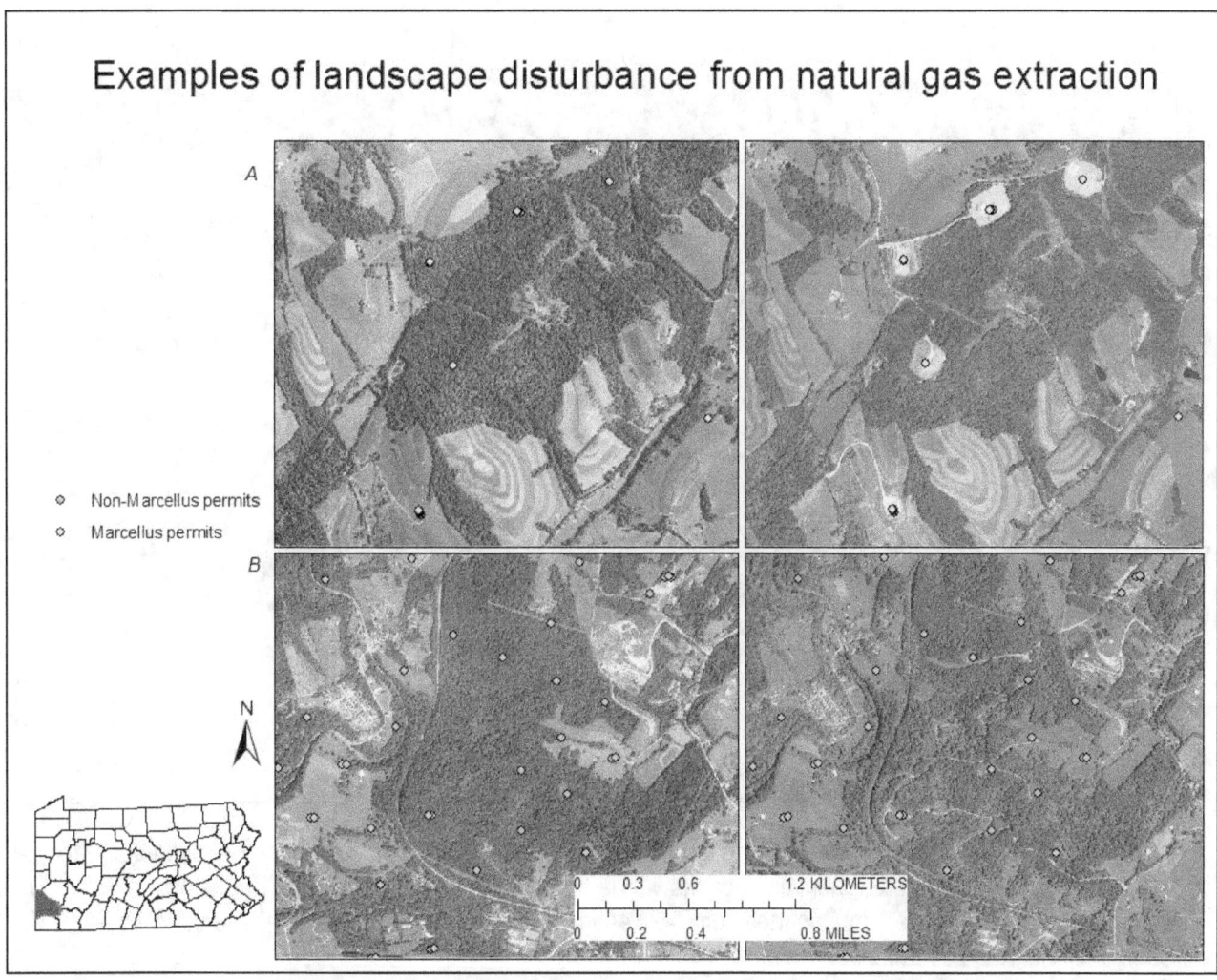

Figure 2. Example of forested landscapes from Washington County, Pennsylvania, showing the spatial effects of roads, well pads, and pipelines related to (*A*) Marcellus Shale and (*B*) Conventional natural gas development. Inset shows the location of the images. Base-map data courtesy of *The National Map* [(*http://viewer.nationalmap.gov/viewer) (U.S.* Geological Survey, 2011a)].

Location

This assessment of landscape effects focuses on two counties, Lackawanna County and Wayne County in Pennsylvania, within the Marcellus Shale area of development known as the "Marcellus Shale Play" Or the Interior Marcellus Shale AU. These counties were chosen for their position adjacent to a "sweet spot" of exceptionally productive Marcellus Shale (Stevens and Kuuskraa, 2009). Figure 3 identifies the selected counties in relation to the Interior Marcellus Shale AU and the distribution of Marcellus and non-Marcellus gas extraction permits granted by Pennsylvania.

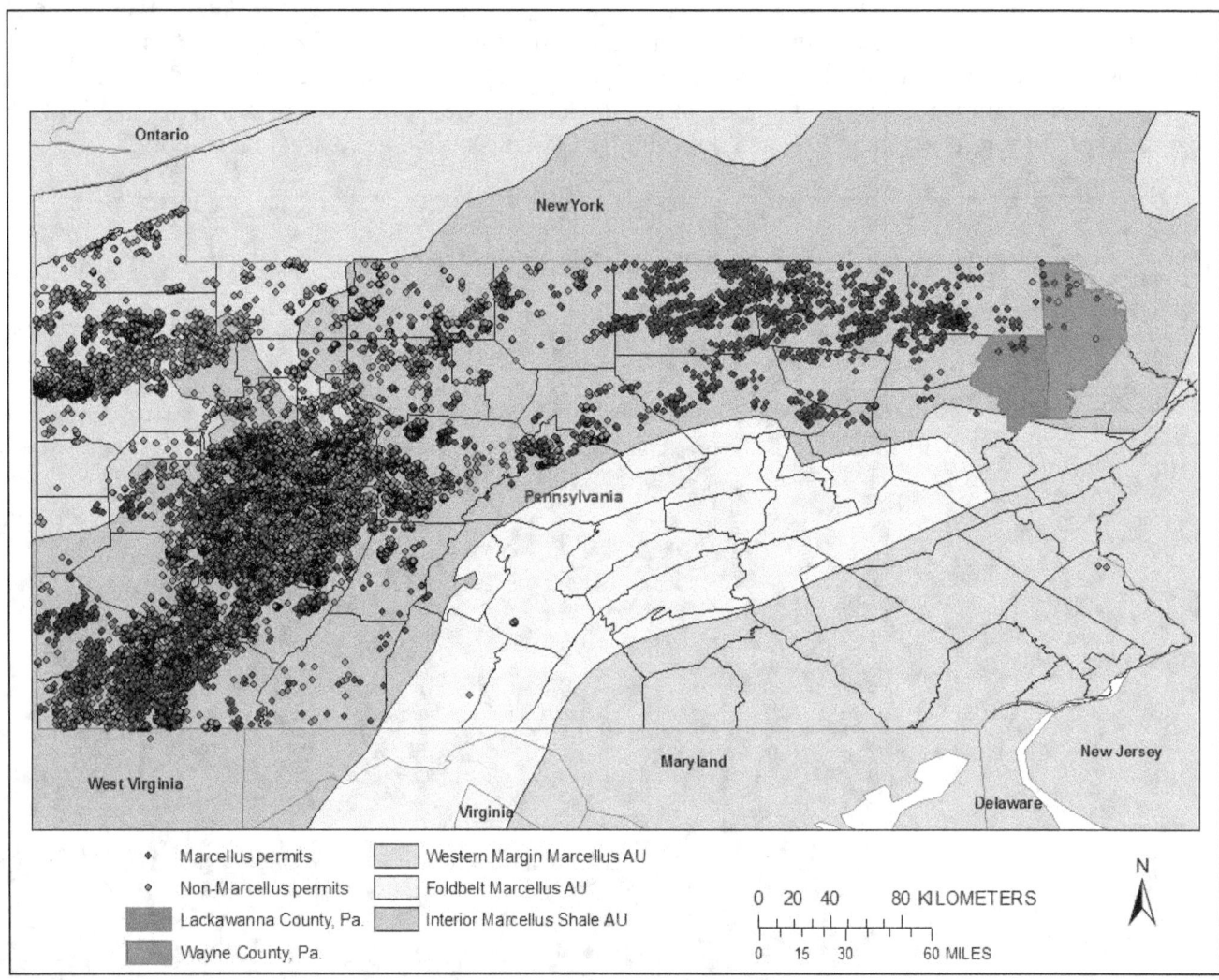

Figure 3. The distribution of Marcellus and non-Marcellus natural gas permits issued between 2004 and 2010 within Pennsylvania, the focal counties of Lackawanna and Wayne, and their relation to the interior Marcellus Shale assessment unit. Base-map data courtesy of *The National Map* [(*http://viewer.nationalmap.gov/viewer*) (U.S. Geological Survey, 2011a)].

The Biogeography of Pennsylvania Forests

Forests are a critical land cover in Pennsylvania. Prior to the European settlements, Pennsylvania was almost completely forested and even today, with modern agriculture, urban growth, and population growth, Pennsylvania is still roughly 60 percent forested. Pennsylvania forests of the 17th century were diverse but were dominated by beech and hemlock, which composed 65 percent of the total forest (Pennsylvania Department of Conservation and Natural Resources, 2011). In the late 19th century, Pennsylvania became the country's leading source of lumber, and a number of products, from lumber to the production of tannic acid, were generated from the forestry industry (Pennsylvania Department of Conservation and Natural Resources, 2011). By the early 20th century, most of Pennsylvania's forests had been harvested. Soon after most of the trees were felled, wildfires, erosion, and flooding became prevalent, especially in the Allegheny Plateau region (Pennsylvania Parks and Forests Foundation, 2010).

The 20th century saw resurgence in Pennsylvania forests. The Weeks Act of 1911 authorized the Federal purchase of forest land on the headwaters of navigable rivers to control the flow of water downstream and act as a measure of flood control for the thriving steel industry of Pittsburgh. Slowly, the forests began to grow back but with a vastly different composition, this time composed of black cherry, red maple, and sugar maple species (Pennsylvania Parks and Forests Foundation, 2010). For the most part, except for a few isolated areas in north central Pennsylvania and some State parks, the majority of forest cover is currently of the new composition and not of virgin forest. Figure 4 shows that today the concentrations of forests in Pennsylvania are highest in the central and north-central parts of the State, which is also the main area of hydraulic-fracturing activity in the Marcellus Shale.

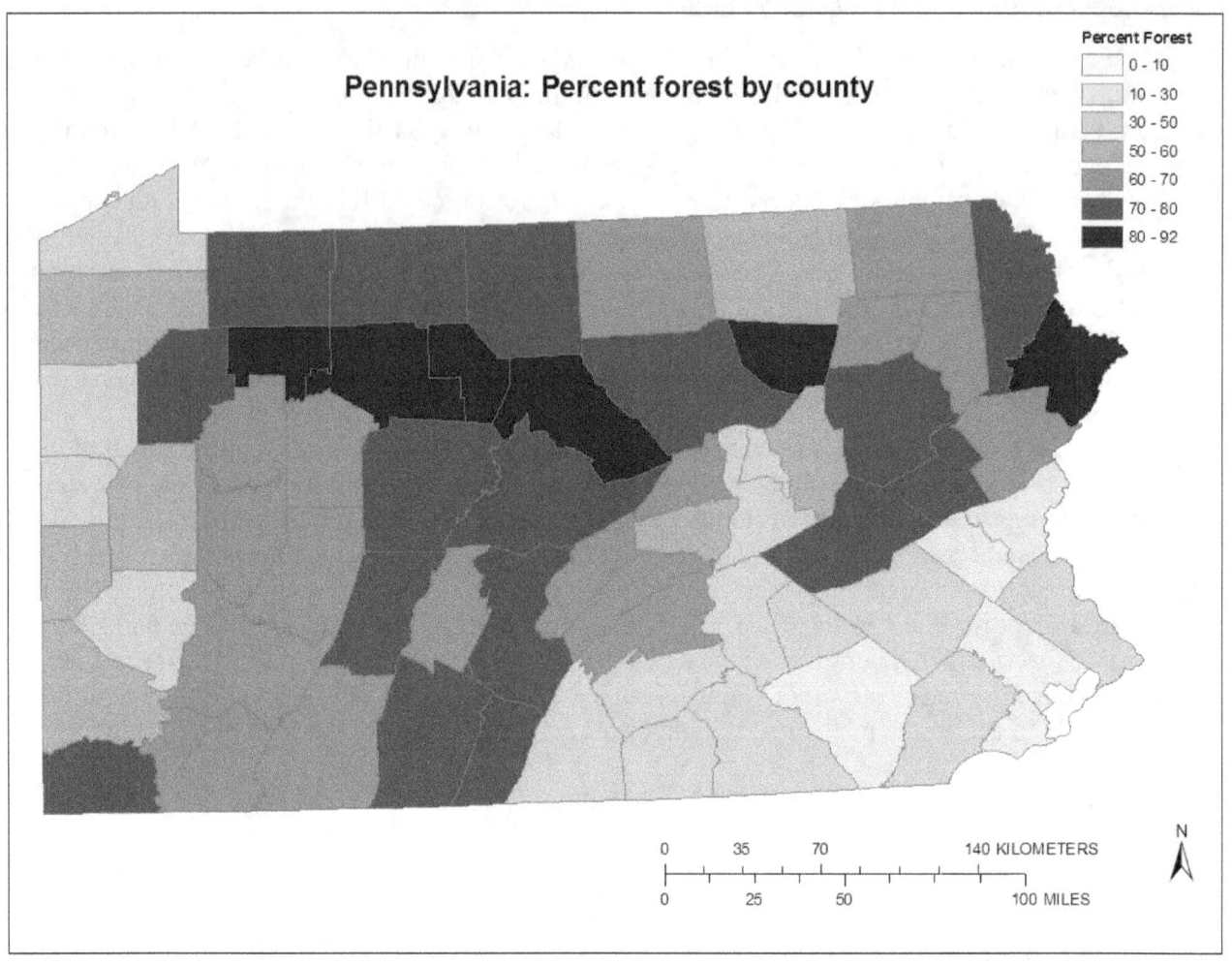

Figure 4. The distribution of percent forest cover by county based on the U.S. Geological Survey 2001 National Land Cover Data. Base-map data courtesy of *The National Map* [(*http://viewer.nationalmap.gov/viewer*) (U.S. Geological Survey, 2011a)].

Pennsylvania forests provide critical habitat to a number of plant and animal species. Plant species include the sugar maple, the eastern redcedar, and evergreens that produce berries in the winter. There were a number of animal species that have been eradicated from the region, such as elk, moose, North American cougar, bison, and grey wolf (Nilsson, 2005). Today, animal species range from the more commonly found animals, such as skunks to flying squirrels, and multiple different varieties of snakes and bats. However, a diverse population of birds depends on the forests for survival. In the State of Pennsylvania, there are 394 different bird species that are native, including endangered species such as the piping plover (Gross, 2005).

Key Research Questions

An important aspect of this research was to quantify the level of disturbance in terms of land use and land cover change by specific disturbance category (well pads, roads, pipelines, and so forth). This quantification was accomplished by extracting the signatures of disturbance from high-resolution aerial images and then computing landscape metrics in a geographic information system (GIS) environment.

This research and monitoring effort focused on answering the following key questions:

- What is the level of overall disturbance attributed to gas exploration and development activities and how has this changed over time?
- What are the structural components (land cover classes) of this change and how much change can be attributed to each class?
- How has the disturbance associated with natural gas exploration and development affected the structure, pattern, and process of key ecosystems, especially forests, within the Marcellus Shale Play?
- How will the disturbance stressors affect ecosystem structure and function at a landscape and watershed scale?

Landscape Metrics and a Landscape Perspective

An important and sometimes overlooked aspect of contemporary gas exploration activity is the geographic profile and spatial arrangement of these activities on the land surface. The function of ecosystems and the services they provide are due in large part to their spatial arrangement on the landscape. Energy exploration and development represents a specific form of land use and land cover change (LULCC) activity that substantially alters certain critical aspects of the spatial pattern, form, and function of landscape interactions.

Changes in land use and land cover affect the ability of ecosystems to provide essential ecological goods and services, which, in turn, affect the economic, public health, and social benefits that these ecosystems provide. One of the great challenges for geographic science is to understand and calibrate the effects of LULCC and the complex interaction between human and biotic systems at a variety of natural, geographic, and political scales (Slonecker and others, 2010).

Changes in land use and land cover, such as the disturbance and the landscape effects of energy exploration, are currently occurring at a relatively rapid pace that is prompting immediate scientific focus and attention. Understanding the dynamics of land surface change requires an increased understanding of the complex nature of human-environmental systems and requires a suite of scientific tools that include traditional geographic data and analysis methods, such as remote sensing and GIS, as well as innovative approaches to understanding the dynamics of complex natural systems (O'Neill and others, 1997; Turner, 2005; Wickham and others, 2007). One such approach that has gained much recent scientific attention is the landscape indicator, or landscape assessment, approach, which has been developed within the science of landscape ecology (O'Neill and others, 1997).

Landscape assessment utilizes spatially explicit imagery; GIS data on land cover, elevation, roads, hydrology, vegetation; and in situ sampling results to compute a suite of numerical indicators known as **landscape metrics** to assess ecosystem condition. Landscape analysis is focused on the relation between pattern and process and broad-scale ecological relationships such as habitat, conservation, and sustainability. Landscape analysis necessarily considers both biological and socioeconomic issues and relationships. This research explores these relationships and their potential effect on various ecosystems and biological endpoints within the context of natural gas exploration.

The landscape assessment presented here is based largely on the framework outlined in O'Neill and others (1997). Many landscape metrics can be computed and utilized for some analytical purpose. However, it has been shown by several researchers (Riitters and others, 1995; Wickham and Riitters, 1995; Wickham and others, 1997) that many of these metrics are highly correlated, sensitive to misclassification and pixel size, and, to some extent, questionable in terms of additional information value. The key landscape concepts and metrics reported here are discussed below. The actual formulae used to compute these specific metrics can be found in software documentation for FRAGSTATS (McGarigal and others, 2002) and Analytical Tools Interface for Landscape Assessments (ATtILA)

(Ebert and Wade, 2004). Computation details for percent interior forest and percent edge forest are documented by Riitters and others (2000).

The concept of landscape metrics, sometimes called landscape indices, is derived from the field of landscape ecology and is rooted in the realization that pattern and structure are important components of ecological process. Landscape metrics are spatial/mathematical indices allow the objective description of different aspects of landscape structures and patterns (McGarigal and others, 2002). Landscape metrics characterize the landscape structure and various processes at both landscape and ecosystem levels. Metrics such as average patch size, fragmentation, and interior forest dimension capture spatial characteristics of habitat quality and potential change effects on critical animal and vegetation populations.

Two different geostatistical landscape analysis programs were used to measure the landscape metrics presented in this report. FRAGSTATS (University of Massachusetts, Amherst, Mass.) is a spatial pattern analysis program for quantifying numerous landscape metrics and their distribution, and is available at *http://www.umass.edu/landeco/research/fragstats/fragstats.html* (McGarigal and others, 2002). ATtILA (U.S. Environmental Protection Agency (USEPA), Las Vegas, Nev.) is an Esri (Environmental Systems Research Institute, Redlands, Calif.) Arcview 3.x extension that computes a number of landscape, riparian, and watershed metrics and is available at *http://www.epa.gov/esd/land-sci/attila/* (Ebert and Wade, 2004). Metrics are presented here at the county level and mapped at the watershed level defined by 12-digit Hydrologic Unit Codes (HUC-12).

Disturbance

Disturbance is a key concept in a landscape analysis approach and in ecology in general. Gas development activities create a number of disturbances across a heterogeneous landscape. In landscape analysis, disturbances are discrete events in space and time that disrupt ecosystem structure and function and change resource availability and the physical environment (White and Pickett, 1985; Turner and others, 2001). When natural or anthropogenic disturbance occurs in natural systems, it generally alters abiotic and biotic conditions that favor the success of different species, such as opportunistic invasive species over predisturbance organisms. Natural gas exploration and development result in spatially explicit patterns of landscape disturbance involving the construction of well pads and impoundments, roads, pipelines, and disposal activities that have structural impacts on the landscape (fig. 2).

Development of multiple sources of natural gas results in increased traffic from construction, drilling operations (horizontal and vertical), hydraulic fracturing, extraction, transportation, and maintenance activities. The presence of humans, construction machinery, infrastructure (for example, well pads and pipelines), roads, and vehicles alone may substantially impact flora and fauna. Increased traffic, especially rapid increases on roads that have historically received little activity, can have detrimental impacts on animal and plant populations (Gibbs and Shriver, 2005). Forest loss as a result of disturbance, fragmentation, and edge effects has been shown to negatively affect water quality and runoff (Wickham and others, 2008), impact species, alter biosphere-atmosphere dynamics that could contribute to climate change (Hayden, 1998; Bonan, 2008), and affect the long-term survival of the forest itself (Gascon and others, 2007).

The initial step of landscape analysis is to determine the spatial distribution of disturbance to identify relative hotspots of activity. This knowledge allows greater focus to be placed on specific locations. Disturbance in this report is presented as both graphic files and tables of summary statistics. Figure 5 provides an example of the distribution of natural gas extraction in Bradford County, Pennsylvania, and it also shows how that disturbance is placed with respect to the local land cover.

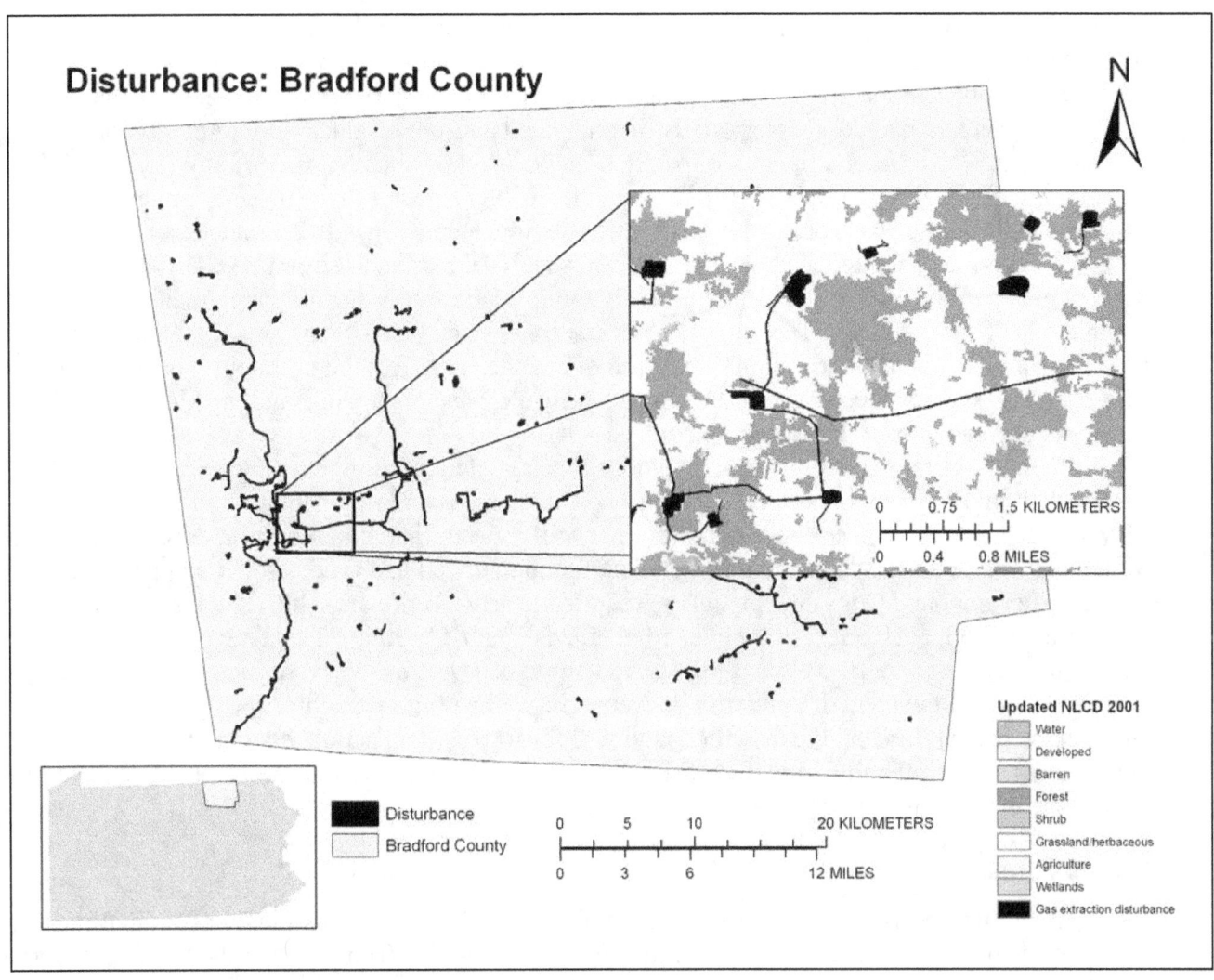

Figure 5. Example of a natural gas disturbance footprint from Bradford County, Pennsylvania, embedded within the National Land Cover Dataset (NLCD) 2001. Base-map data courtesy of *The National Map* [(*http://viewer.nationalmap.gov/viewer*) (*U.S.* Geological Survey, 2011a)].

Forest Fragmentation

Forest fragmentation is the alteration of forest into smaller, less functional areas. Fragmentation of forest and habitat is a primary concern resulting from current gas development. Habitat fragmentation occurs when large areas of natural landscapes are intersected and subdivided by other, usually anthropogenic, land uses leaving smaller patches to serve as habitat for various species. As human activities increase, natural habitats, such as forests, are divided into smaller and smaller patches that have a decreased ability to support viable populations of individual species, particularly those in large ranges adapted to interior forest conditions. Habitat loss and forest fragmentation can be major threats to biodiversity, although research on this topic is inconclusive (With and Pavuk, 2011).

Although many human and natural activities result in habitat fragmentation, gas exploration and development activity can be extreme in their effect on the landscape. The development of numerous secondary roads and pipeline networks crisscrosses and subdivides habitat structure.

Landscape disturbance associated with shale-gas development infrastructure directly alters habitat through loss, fragmentation, and edge effects, which in turn alter the flora and fauna dependent on that habitat. The fragmentation of habitat is expected to amplify the problem of total habitat area reduction for wildlife species, as well as contribute to habitat degradation. Fragmentation alters the landscape by creating a mosaic of spatially distinct habitats from originally contiguous habitat, resulting in smaller patch size, greater number of patches, and decreased interior to edge ratio (Lehmkuhl and Ruggiero, 1991; Dale and others, 2000). Fragmented habitats generally result in detrimental impacts to flora and fauna caused by increased mortality of individuals moving between patches, lower recolonization rates, and reduced local population sizes (Fahrig and Merriam, 1994). The remaining patches may be too small, isolated, and possibly too influenced by edge effects to maintain viable populations of some species. The rate of landscape change can be more important than the amount or type of change because the temporal dimension of change can affect the probability of recolonization for endemic species, which are typically restricted by their dispersal range and the kinds of landscapes in which they can move (Fahrig and Merriam, 1994).

While general assumptions and hypotheses can be derived from existing scientific literature involving similar stressors, the specific impacts of habitat loss and fragmentation in the Marcellus Shale Play will depend on the needs and attributes of specific species and communities. A recent analysis of Marcellus well permit locations in Pennsylvania found that well pads and associated infrastructure (roads, water impoundments, and pipelines) required nearly 3.6 hectares (ha) (9 acres) per well pad with an additional 8.5 ha (21 acres) of indirect edge effects (Johnson, 2010). This type of extensive and long-term habitat conversion has a greater impact on natural ecosystems than activities such as logging or agriculture, given the great dissimilarity between gas-well pad infrastructure and adjacent natural areas and the low probability that the disturbed land will revert back to a natural state in the near future (high persistence) (Marzluff and Ewing, 2001). Figure 6 shows an example of the concept of the landscape metric of forest fragmentation.

Interior Forest

Interior forest is a special form of habitat that is preferred by many plant and animal species and is defined as the area of forest at least 100 m from the forest edge (Harper and others, 2005). Interior forest is an important landscape characteristic because the environmental conditions, such as light, wind, humidity, and exposure to predators, within the interior forest are different from areas closer to the forest edge. Interior forest habitat is related to the size and distribution of forest patches and is closely tied to the concept of forest or habitat **fragmentation**. The amount of interior forest can be dramatically affected by linear land use patterns, such as roads and pipelines, which tend to fragment land patches into several smaller patches and destroy available habitat for certain species. Figure 6 shows the general concept of increased fragmentation and reduced interior forest.

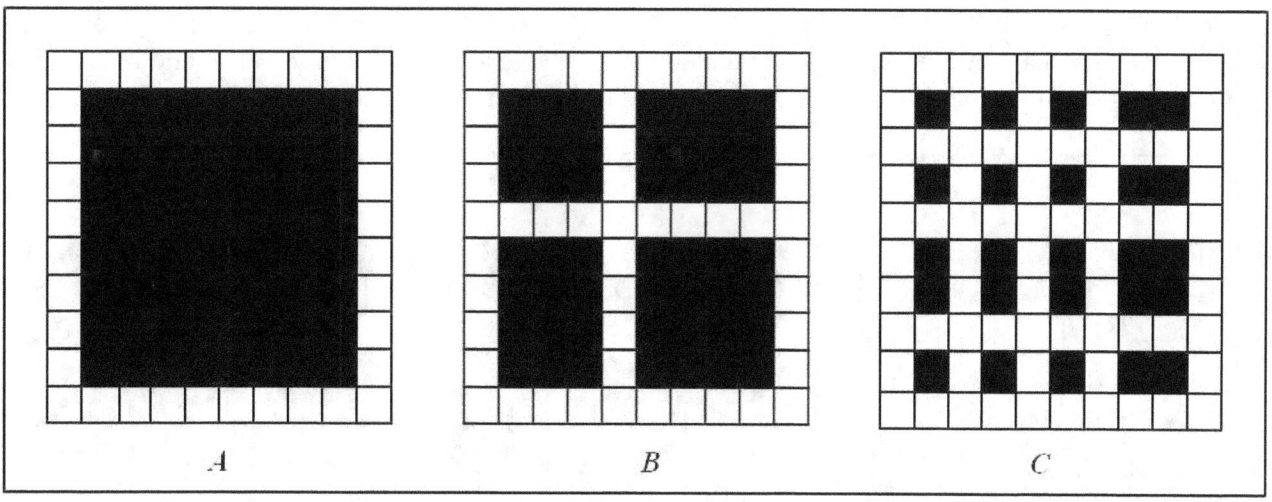

Figure 6.   Conceptual illustration of interior forest and how this critical habitat is affected by linear disturbance. *A,* High interior area; *B,* Moderate interior area; and *C,* Low interior area (Riitters and others, 1996).

Forest Edge

Forest edge is simply a linear measure of the amount of edge between forest and other land uses in a given area, and especially between natural and human-dominated landscapes. The influence of the two bordering communities on each other is known as the edge effect. When edges are expanded into natural ecosystems, and the area outside the boundary is a disturbed or unnatural system, the natural ecosystem can be affected for some distance in from the edge (Skole and Tucker, 1993). Edge effects are variable in space and time. The intensity of edge effects diminishes as one moves deeper inside a forest, but edge phenomena can vary greatly within the same habitat fragment or landscape (Laurance and others, 2007). Factors that might promote edge-effect variability include the age of habitat edges, edge aspect, and the combined effects of multiple nearby edges, fragment size, seasonality, and extreme weather events.

Spatial variability of edge effects may result from local factors such as the proximity and number of nearby forest edges. Plots with two or more neighboring edges, such as smaller fragment plots, have greater tree mortality and biomass loss. Edge age also influences edge effects. Over time, forest edge can be partially sealed by invasive vines and second growth underbrush, which will influence the ability of smaller tree seedlings to survive in this environment. Likewise, the matrix of adjoining vegetation plots will have a strong influence on edge effects. Forest edges adjoined by young regrowth forest provide a physical buffer from wind and light. Extreme weather events also affect the temporal variability in edge effects. Abrupt, artificial boundaries of forest fragments are vulnerable to windstorms, snow and ice, and convectional thunderstorms that can weaken and destroy exposed forest edges. Periodic droughts can also have a more pronounced effect on forest edges that are exposed to drier wind conditions and higher rates of evaporation.

Contagion

Contagion is an indicator that measures the degree of "clumpiness" among the classes of land cover features and is related to patch size and distribution. Contagion ($0 < x \leq 100$, disaggregated to aggregated) expresses the degree to which adjacent pixel pairs can be found in the landscape. Figure 7 shows the general concept of contagion and gives examples of low, medium, and high contagion.

Contagion is valuable because it relates an important measure of how landscapes are fragmented by patches. Landscapes of large, less-fragmented patches have a high contagion value, and landscapes of numerous small patches have a low contagion value (McGarigal and others, 2002).

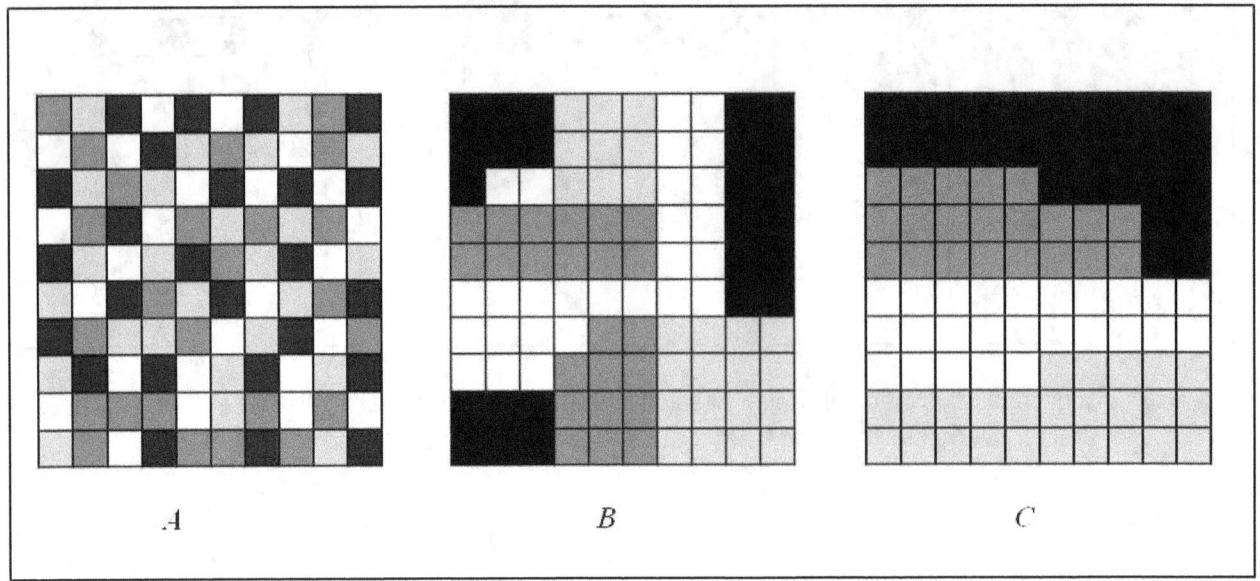

Figure 7. The concept of contagion is the degree to which similar land cover pixels are adjacent or "clumped" to one another. *A,* Low contagion; *B,* Moderate contagion; and *C,* High contagion (after Riitters and others, 1996).

Fractal Dimension

Fractal dimension describes the complexity of patches or edges within a landscape and is generally related to the level of anthropogenic influence in a landscape. Fractal dimension generally measures the perimeter-to-area proportional relationship of a patch. Human land uses tend to have simple circular or rectangular shapes of low complexity and, therefore, low fractal dimensions. Natural land covers have irregular edges, complex arrangements and, therefore, higher fractal dimensions. The fractal dimension index ranges between 1 and 2, with 1 indicating high human influences in the landscape and 2 with natural patterns and low human influence (McGarigal and others, 2002).

Dominance

Dominance is a measure of the relative abundance of different patch types, typically emphasizing either relative evenness or equity in the distribution. Dominance is high when one land cover type occupies a relatively large area of a given landscape and is low when land cover types are evenly distributed. Dominance is the complement to evenness, which is sometimes used as an alternative measure of the relative area of one land cover type over others in the landscape.

Although there are many metrics associated with dominance, here we report on a simple landscape metric—the Simpson's Evenness Index, which is a measure of the proportion of the landscape occupied by a patch type divided by the total number of patch types in the landscape (McGarigal and others, 2002).

Methodology: Mapping and Measuring Disturbance Effects

High-resolution aerial imagery for each of four timeframes—2004, 2005/2006, 2008, and 2010—were brought into a geographic information system (GIS) database, along with additional geospatial data on Marcellus and non-Marcellus well permits and locations, administrative boundaries, ecoregions, and geospatial information on the footprint of the Marcellus Shale Play in Pennsylvania. The imagery was examined for distinct signs of disturbance related to oil and gas drilling and development as described below. The observable features were manually digitized as line and polygon features in a GIS format. The polygons and line features were processed and aggregated into a raster mask used to update existing land cover data. Summary statistics for each county were developed and reported. Detailed landscape metrics were calculated and mapped over HUC-12 watersheds within or intersecting the boundary of each county. All metrics are calculated on the 2001 NLCD and the 2001 NLCD as updated by disturbance collected from 2004 to 2010 to isolate the natural gas extraction disturbance effects.

Data

Sources

High-resolution aerial imagery (1 m) from the National Agricultural Imagery Program (NAIP) was downloaded for each timeframe. NAIP imagery is flown to analyze the status of agricultural lands approximately every 2 to 3 years (U.S. Department of Agriculture, Farm Service Agency, 2011). The NAIP imagery consists of readily available, high-resolution data that are suitable for detailed analysis of the landscape. NAIP imagery is available from the U.S. Department of Agriculture Geospatial Data Gateway Web site (U.S. Department of Agriculture, Natural Resources Conservation Service, 2011). Table 1 identifies the source imagery dates for each county and year.

Table 1. Acquisition dates of National Agriculture Imagery Program (NAIP) source data.

Year	Source Imagery Dates (chronological from left to right)			
	Lackawanna County			
2004	2004-08-23	2004-09-01	2004-09-20	2004-10-03
2005	2005-06-24	2005-07-10		
2006				
2008	2008-06-13	2008-09-04	2008-09-05	2008-10-10
2010	2010-07-11	2010-08-07	2010-09-01	
	Wayne County			
2004	2004-08-23	2004-09-01	2004-09-20	2004-10-03
2005	2005-06-24	2005-07-10	2005-07-11	2005-07-24
2006				
2008	2008-06-10	2008-06-12	2008-06-13	2008-09-04
2010	2010-08-07			

Drilling permits for Marcellus Shale and non-Marcellus Shale natural gas were obtained from the Pennsylvania Department of Environmental Protection Permit and Rig Activity Reports for 2004–2010 (Pennsylvania Department of Environmental Protection, Office of Oil and Gas Management, 2011).

The U.S. Geological Survey (USGS) Watershed Boundary Dataset 12-digit Hydrologic Unit Code (HUC-12) for Pennsylvania was downloaded from the USGS National Hydrography Dataset Web site (U.S. Geological Survey, 2011b).

The Marcellus Shale Play assessment unit boundaries were downloaded from the USGS Energy Resources Program Data Services Web site (U.S. Geological Survey, 2012).

The 2001 National Land Cover Dataset (NLCD) was acquired for use as the baseline land cover map. The NLCD is a 16-class land cover classification scheme applied consistently across the United States at a 30-m spatial resolution (Homer and others, 2007) and is released on a 5-year cycle. The 2001 NLCD was chosen as the baseline because the 2006 NLCD contained some of the landscape changes collected during this study. The NLCD may be acquired using the Multi-Resolution Land Characteristics Consortium Web site (U.S. Geological Survey, 2011c). The NLCD 2001 was resampled to 10-m-pixel size.

Collection

These data were brought into a GIS database for spatial analysis. The imagery was examined for distinct signs of disturbance related to oil and gas drilling and development. These features include the following:

- Sites—Cleared areas related to existing permits or displaying the characteristics of a shale or conventional gas extraction site.
- Roads—Vehicular transportation corridors constructed specifically for shale or conventional gas development.
- Pipelines—New gas pipelines constructed in conjunction with one or more well pads.
- Impoundments—Manmade depressions designed to hold liquid and in support of oil and gas drilling operations.
- Other—Support areas or activities such as processing plants, storage tanks, and staging areas.

The collection of gas extraction infrastructure data was a manual process of visually examining high-resolution imagery for each county over four dates to identify and digitize (collect) changes in the land cover resulting from the development of gas extraction infrastructure. Specifically, NAIP 1-m data composited for the years 2004, 2005/2006, 2008, and 2010 were examined using 2004 imagery as a baseline, identifying landscape changes that occurred after 2004.

Changes that correlated with natural gas extraction permits, appeared to be natural gas extraction related or were in proximity to other gas extraction infrastructure were selected and digitized to the maximum extent of landscape disturbance. The focus of the data collection was on features attributable to the construction, use, and maintenance of gas extraction drill sites, processing plants, and compressor stations, as well as the center lines for new roads accessing such sites, plants, and stations, and the center lines for new pipelines used to transport the extracted gas. Figure 8 shows examples of digitized natural gas extraction features. These data were collected within shapefiles by county, using ArcGIS 10.0. One shapefile was generated for sites (polygons), one was generated for roads (lines), and one was generated for pipelines (lines). Roads and pipelines were generally buffered to 8 and 12 m, respectively, for overall area assessments. The buffered distance was selected as the average from measurement of roads and pipelines in the counties. All sites were initially classified as gas extraction related or points of interest. Points of interest were unlikely to be related to drilling, but were of potential future interest and excluded from further processing. All data collected were reviewed by another team member for concurrence and consistency.

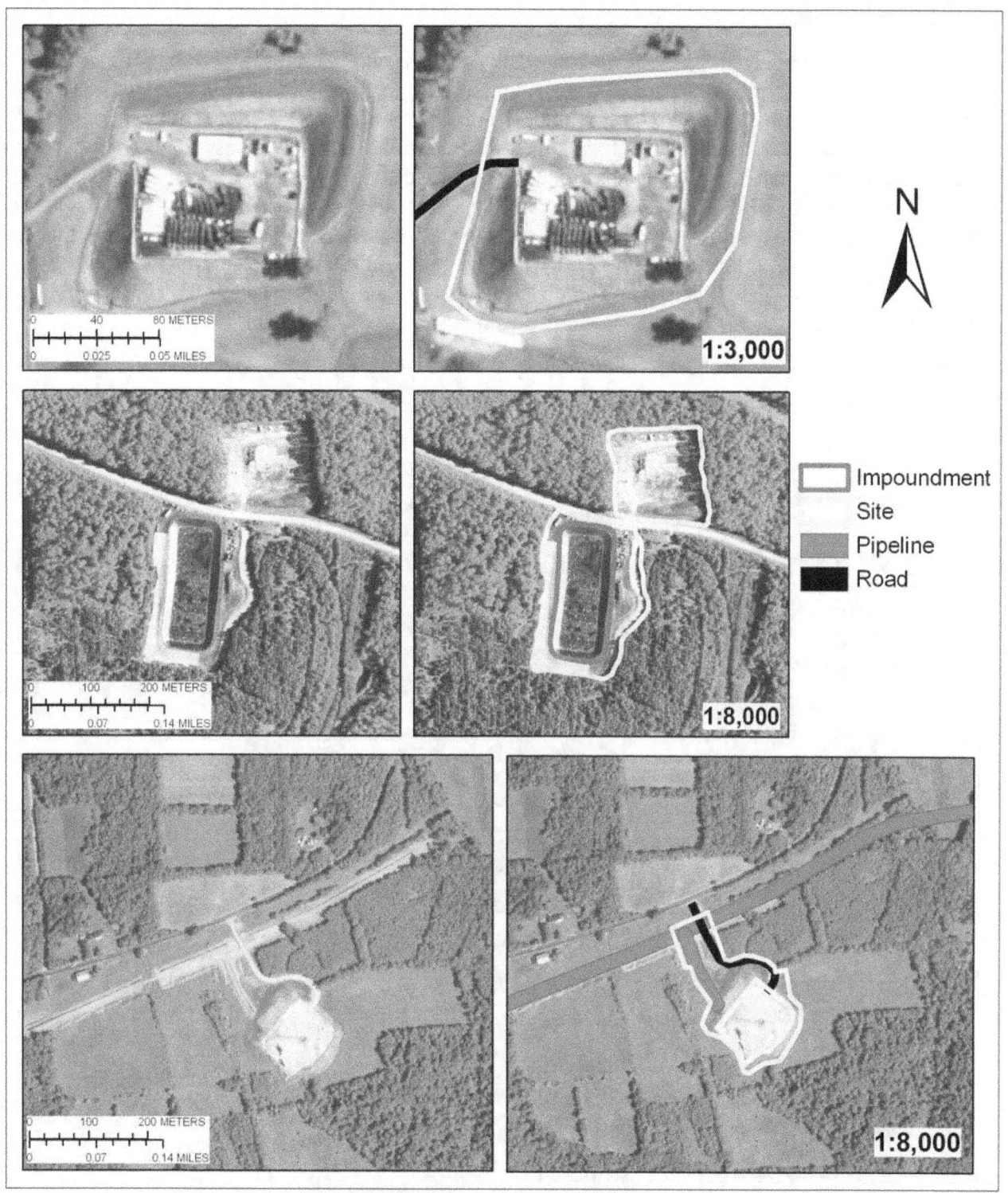

Figure 8. Examples of spatially explicit features of disturbance that were extracted from aerial photographs into a geographic information system (GIS) format.

Land Cover Update

Using the collected and reviewed data, the polygons and line features were processed and aggregated into a raster format used as a mask to update existing land cover data from NLCD 2001. Figure 9 shows the processing flow to accomplish this task consistently across both counties.

Each feature within the shapefiles was compared to the permit database to determine its permit status and its area calculated. A subset of features and roads was selected by infrastructure type (all, Marcellus, non-Marcellus, other and pipelines). The selected features were then merged and internal boundaries dissolved resulting in a disturbance footprint shapefile for that county. The disturbance footprint was then rasterized (10-m-pixel size)and used to conditionally select the pixels in the resampled 2001 NLCD to reclassify as a new class: gas extraction disturbance. To consistently perform this processing, a set of models was developed using the ArcGIS ModelBuilder.

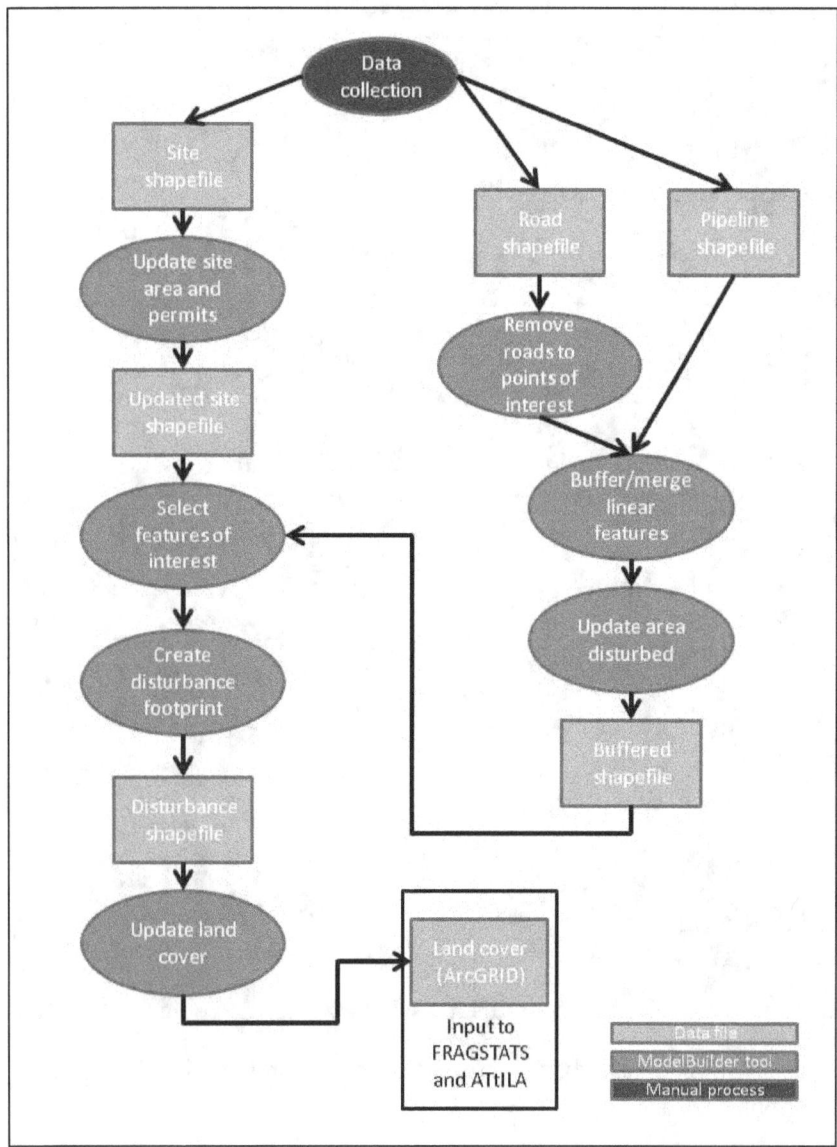

Figure 9. Workflow diagram for creating an updated land cover map. The workflow was implemented using ArcGIS ModelBuilder scripts to process the digitized data and embed results in the resampled NLCD 2001.

Calculation of Landscape Metrics

Landscape-wide and land cover class fragmentation statistics for each county were developed and reported using FRAGSTATS, while land cover class-detailed statistics, forest fragmentation statistics, including patch metrics and forest condition (interior, edge, and so forth) metrics were calculated over smaller watersheds (HUC12) intersecting with the county using ATtILA. The collected statistics were then summarized, charted, and mapped for further analysis.

In addition to the summary of features noted above, a series of landscape metrics was calculated for each county based on the change related to gas development activities between 2004 and 2010. To do this, the metrics were calculated from the 2001 NLCD dataset (Homer and others, 2007). Following that calculation, the 2004–2010 cumulative spatial pattern of disturbance was digitally embedded into the 2001 NLCD dataset and the metrics were recalculated for each county.

Results: Summary Statistics and Graphics

This section presents a summary for each county of landscape alterations from natural gas resource development, along with the ensuing change in land cover and landscape metrics using metrics suggested by O'Neill and others (1997). These metrics are then calculated and presented based on the sources of that disturbance: Marcellus (MS) sites and roads; non-Marcellus (non-MS) (conventional) sites and roads; other infrastructure, which includes nonpermitted sites, processing facilities and their associated roads; and pipelines and their associated roads. Nonpermitted sites are defined as disturbed areas that appear to be Marcellus or non-Marcellus gas extraction sites that do not have a permit within 250 m of the disturbance. These data are presented in tabular form with some graphic presentations provided where appropriate. Examples of the spatial distribution of selected landscape metrics are shown at the watershed level for each county. GIS data of all disturbance features are available upon request.

Disturbed Area

Documenting the spatially explicit patterns of disturbance was one of the primary goals of this research, and this section describes the extent of disturbed land cover for Lackawanna and Wayne Counties in Pennsylvania. The spatial distribution of disturbance influences the impacts of that disturbance. Figure 10 shows the distribution of disturbance within Lackawanna and Wayne Counties.

In Lackawanna County, disturbance is a single Marcellus site located near the northern county boundary. In Wayne County, disturbance is dispersed in the northern third and is primarily Marcellus Shale natural gas extraction. The detailed insets in figure 10 show the disturbance footprints in the context of the surrounding land cover.

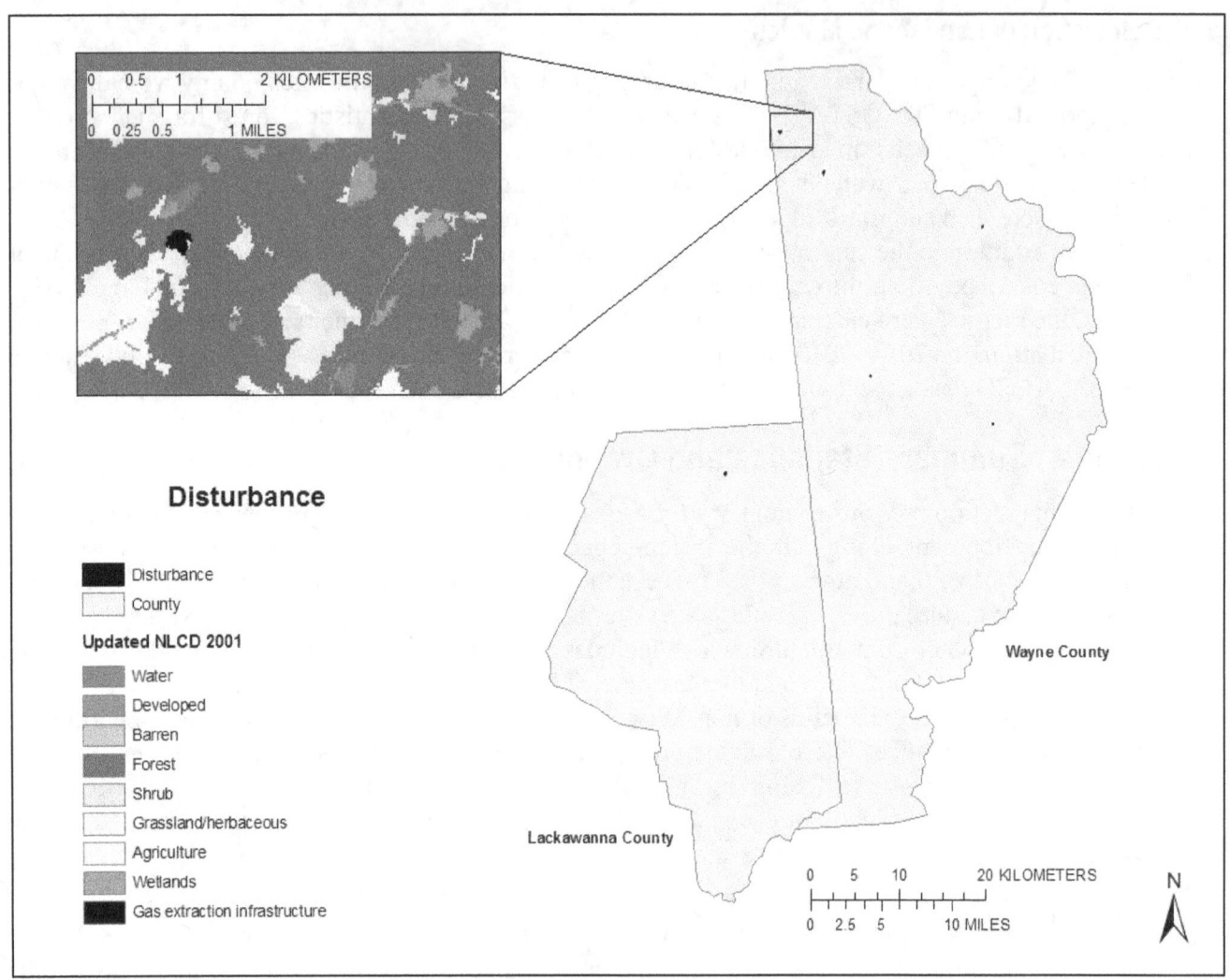

Figure 10. Gas extraction-related disturbance identified between 2004 and 2010 in Lackawanna and Wayne Counties, Pennsylvania. Base-map data courtesy of *The National Map* [(*http://viewer.nationalmap.gov/viewer*) (U.S. Geological Survey, 2011a)].

Table 2 lists the disturbance area attributable to all sites and impoundments and their associated roads and pipelines. The disturbance area is presented first as a total disturbance for all gas extraction infrastructure, including all sites, roads, and pipelines. Total disturbance is then divided into sections: the first includes disturbance for all sites and their associated roads and the second includes disturbance for pipelines and impoundments. The disturbance area for all sites and roads is further divided into disturbance for Marcellus Shale permitted sites and roads, non-Marcellus Shale permitted sites and roads, sites lacking an identifiable permit (for example, processing facilities or incomplete permit data), and sites with permits for both Marcellus and non-Marcellus drilling, also called dual sites. Additionally, the disturbance area associated with impoundments is presented for those impoundments greater than 0.4 ha and for those less than 0.4 ha. Because land disturbance or access roads may be associated with multiple infrastructural components (for example, pipelines may cross areas also disturbed for drill sites), the values for disturbed areas and road miles within break-out categories such as "MS sites and roads," do not sum up to the higher level category—in this instance "All sites and

18

roads." The results indicate the following changes occurred based on 2004–2010 natural gas development:

- Lackawanna County had one Marcellus site developed between 2004 and 2010.
- Wayne County had five sites developed—three Marcellus, one non-Marcellus, and one other.

Table 2. Cumulative landscape disturbance for natural gas extraction development and infrastructure based on disturbance type from 2004 to 2010 by county.

[Note: Categories are not mutually exclusive. MS, Marcellus Shale site; non-MS, non-Marcellus Shale site; >, greater than; <, less than; ha, hectare]

Land cover update	Count	Site only hectares	Footprint disturbed hectares	Road kilometers	Pipeline kilometers	Hectares per site	Disturbed hectares per site	Road kilometers per site
Lackawanna County (120,461 ha)								
All infrastructure	1	4.9	5.0	0.5	0.0	4.9	5.0	0.5
All sites and roads	1	4.9	5.0	0.5		4.9		
MS sites and roads	1	4.9	5.0	0.5		4.9	5.0	0.5
Non-MS sites and roads	0							
Other infrastructure/ nonpermitted sites and roads	0							
Dual sites	0							
Pipelines	0							
Impoundments (>0.4 ha)	2	1.3				0.6		
Impoundments (<0.4 ha)	0							
Wayne County (196,415 ha)								
All infrastructure	5	15.8	16.2	2.2	0.0	3.2	3.2	0.4
All sites and roads	5	15.8				3.2	0.0	0.0
MS sites and roads	3	12.3	12.7	1.8		4.1	4.2	0.6
Non-MS sites and roads	1	0.5	0.5	0.2		0.5	0.5	0.2
Other infrastructure/ nonpermitted sites and roads	1	3	3	0.4		3.0	3.0	0.4
Dual sites								
Pipelines	0							
Impoundments (>0.4 ha)	0							
Impoundments (<0.4 ha)	1	0.3				0.3		

Land cover change is the initial impact of disturbance and can have long-term effects on ecological integrity and functions. Table 3 lists the percent land cover by county for 2001 and percent land cover and change for the updated 2010 landscape. The land cover change for the updated landscape is further divided into the values attributable to Marcellus sites; non-Marcellus sites; other infrastructure including nonpermitted sites; and pipelines, each with their associated roads. Given that the natural land cover of Pennsylvania is forest (Kuchler, 1964), the 2001 land cover provides a measure of the impacts prior to most natural gas resource development; the changes between 2004 and 2010 have increased these impacts. Of particular interest are the forest cover and its relation to the critical value 59.28 percent from percolation theory (Gardner and others, 1987; O'Neill and others, 1997). Below this value, the landscape structure rapidly breaks down into isolated patches, thereby changing forest resilience and habitat corridors. The results indicate the following changes occurred based on 2004–2010 natural gas development:

- In both Lackawanna and Wayne Counties, the primary land covers are forest (61 percent and 69 percent, respectively), agriculture (12 percent and 17 percent, respectively), and developed (16 percent and 6 percent, respectively).
- Both Lackawanna and Wayne Counties had greater than the critical amount of forest. That forest showed no effects from the small amount of natural gas development.

Table 3. Percent land cover (2001) and land cover change (2004–2010) presented for each county.

[MS, Marcellus Shale site; non-MS, non-Marcellus Shale site; N/A, Not Applicable—no such infrastructure]

Land Cover	Original land cover	Updated with all infra-structure	Change	Updated with MS sites and roads	Change	Updated with non-MS sites and roads	Change	Updated with other infra-structure and roads	Change	Updated with pipelines and roads	Change
Lackawanna County											
Forest	61.23	61.23	0.00	61.23	0.00	N/A	N/A	N/A	N/A	N/A	N/A
Agriculture	12.39	12.39	0.00	12.39	0.00	N/A	N/A	N/A	N/A	N/A	N/A
Developed	16.33	16.33	0.00	16.33	0.00	N/A	N/A	N/A	N/A	N/A	N/A
Grassland - herbaceous	0.85	0.85	0.00	0.85	0.00	N/A	N/A	N/A	N/A	N/A	N/A
Water	1.79	1.79	0.00	1.79	0.00	N/A	N/A	N/A	N/A	N/A	N/A
Barren	0.42	0.42	0.00	0.42	0.00	N/A	N/A	N/A	N/A	N/A	N/A
Wetlands	4.98	4.98	0.00	4.98	0.00	N/A	N/A	N/A	N/A	N/A	N/A
Scrub - shrub	2.01	2.01	0.00	2.01	0.00	N/A	N/A	N/A	N/A	N/A	N/A
Gas extraction disturbance	0.00	0.00	0.00	0.00	0.00	N/A	N/A	N/A	N/A	N/A	N/A
Wayne County											
Forest	69.06	69.05	0.01	69.05	0.01	69.06	0.00	69.06	0.00	N/A	N/A
Agriculture	16.66	16.65	0.01	16.66	0.00	16.66	0.00	16.66	0.00	N/A	N/A
Developed	5.74	5.74	0.00	5.74	0.00	5.74	0.00	5.74	0.00	N/A	N/A
Grassland - herbaceous	0.63	0.63	0.00	0.63	0.00	0.63	0.00	0.63	0.00	N/A	N/A
Water	2.90	2.90	0.00	2.90	0.00	2.90	0.00	2.90	0.00	N/A	N/A
Barren	0.03	0.03	0.00	0.03	0.00	0.03	0.00	0.03	0.00	N/A	N/A
Wetlands	4.43	4.43	0.00	4.43	0.00	4.43	0.00	4.43	0.00	N/A	N/A
Scrub - shrub	0.55	0.55	0.00	0.55	0.00	0.55	0.00	0.55	0.00	N/A	N/A
Gas extraction disturbance	0.00	0.01	0.01	0.01	0.01	0.00	0.00	0.00	0.00	N/A	N/A

Land Cover Metrics of Interest

There are numerous landscape metrics, many of which are redundant. Table 4 lists the total area, number of patches, total edge, mean fractal index, contagion and evenness metrics for the 2001 county landscape, and the metrics and change for the updated 2010 landscape. The metrics and change for the updated landscape are further divided into the values attributable to Marcellus sites; non-Marcellus sites; other infrastructure, including nonpermitted sites; and pipelines, each with their associated roads. These metrics were chosen for their overall indication of human impacts on the landscape and environmental quality (O'Neill and others, 1997). Increase in the edge, especially between unlike land covers, indicates declining resilience of the natural land cover and movement of species, while the decrease in the mean fractal index ($1\leq x\leq 2$) indicates an increase in human use. Evenness ($0\leq x\leq 1$, where 0 indicates one land cover class and 1 indicates even distribution across land cover classes) indicates the relative heterogeneity of the landscape and is the inverse of the dominance measure (McGarigal and others, 2002) recommended by O'Neill and others (1997). Contagion ($0<x\leq 100$, disaggregated to aggregated) is an indicator that measures the degree of "clumpiness" among the classes of land cover features. The results indicate the following changes occurred based on 2004–2010 natural gas development:

- Total edge increased by 1.2 kilometers (km) and 4.7 km for Lackawanna and Wayne Counties, respectively.
- Fractal index is low for both counties before and after natural gas development, indicating a high level of human influence in these counties.
- Contagion shows a moderate to high level of clumped land cover for both counties.
- Evenness also shows a moderate level of heterogeneity for both counties with no one land cover dominating.
- Evenness has similar values for each infrastructure type in both counties. Given that the expected land cover is forest and an expected evenness value approaching zero, this value indicates a substantially disturbed landscape.

Table 4. Landscape metrics by county for 2001 (original land cover) and as updated for natural gas development disturbance (2004–2010).

[Note: Categories are not mutually exclusive; MS, Marcellus Shale site; non-MS, non-Marcellus Shale site; ha, hectare; km, kilometer; N/A, Not Applicable—no such infrastructure]

Metric	Original land cover	Updated with all infrastructure	Change	Updated with MS sites and roads	Change	Updated with non-MS sites and roads	Change	Updated with other infrastructure and roads	Change	Updated with pipelines and roads	Change
Lackawanna County											
Total area (ha)	120461.0	120461.0	0.0	120461.0	0.0	N/A	N/A	N/A	N/A	N/A	N/A
Total patches	8684	8685	1	8685	1	N/A	N/A	N/A	N/A	N/A	N/A
Total edge (km)	10273.2	10274.4	1.2	10274.4	1.2	N/A	N/A	N/A	N/A	N/A	N/A
Mean fractal index	1.1212	1.1212	0.0000	1.1212	0.0000	N/A	N/A	N/A	N/A	N/A	N/A
Contagion	65.324	67.1735	1.8495	67.1735	1.8495	N/A	N/A	N/A	N/A	N/A	N/A
Evenness	0.6627	0.6523	-0.0104	0.6523	-0.0104	N/A	N/A	N/A	N/A	N/A	N/A
Wayne County											
Total area (ha)	196415.5	196415.5	0.0	196415.5	0.0	196415.5	0.0	196415.5	0.0	N/A	N/A
Total patches	13145	13160	15	13152	7	13147	2	13151	6	N/A	N/A
Total edge (km)	16923.3	16928.1	4.7	16926.9	3.6	16923.7	0.4	16924.1	0.8	N/A	N/A
Mean fractal index	1.1235	1.1235	0.0000	1.1235	0.0000	1.1235	0.0000	1.1235	0.0000	N/A	N/A
Contagion	70.2525	71.83	1.5775	71.8337	1.5812	71.8461	1.5936	71.8431	1.5906	N/A	N/A
Evenness	0.5591	0.5504	-0.0087	0.5504	-0.0087	0.5504	-0.0087	0.5504	-0.0087	N/A	N/A

Forest Fragmentation

Disturbance in the landscape will affect forests by fragmentation, which is the process of dividing large land cover (for example, forest) into smaller segments called patches. A patch is defined as adjacent (forest) pixels, including diagonals. A landscape with many small patches is representative of a highly fragmented landscape. Fragmented forests provide habitat for edge species, but are poor for interior species, and are less likely to provide migration corridors.

Fragmentation may be evaluated by change in the number of patches, and by change in the mean and (or) median patch size. Table 5 compares the changing forest patch metrics for the 2001 land cover, the updated 2010 land cover, and subsets of the updated 2010 land cover based on Marcellus infrastructure, non-Marcellus infrastructure, other infrastructure, and pipelines. The results indicate the following changes occurred based on 2004–2010 natural gas development:

- Forest patch size and number did not change in Lackawanna County.
- Forest patches increased by one in Wayne County. However, Wayne County's mean forest patch size declined by 0.03 ha.
- Both Lackawanna and Wayne have large differences between the forest patch mean area and median area values: 50.93 hectare mean to 0.73 hectare median and 66.98 hectare mean to 0.54 hectare median, respectively. These large differences indicate a skewed population of forest patch sizes, including many small forest patches and few large forest patches.

Table 5. Forest fragmentation metrics by county for 2001 (original land cover) and as updated for natural gas development disturbance (2004–2010).

[Note: Categories are not mutually exclusive; MS, Marcellus Shale site; non-MS, non-Marcellus Shale site; N/A, Not Applicable—no such infrastructure; ha, hectare]

Metric	Original land cover	Updated with all infra-structure	Change	Updated with MS sites and roads	Change	Updated with non-MS sites and roads	Change	Updated with other infra-structure and roads	Change	Updated with pipelines and roads	Change
Lackawanna County											
Number of patches	1448	1448	0.0	1448	0.0	N/A	N/A	N/A	N/A	N/A	N/A
Forest patch mean area (ha)	50.93	50.93	0.00	50.93	0.00	N/A	N/A	N/A	N/A	N/A	N/A
Forest patch median area (ha)	0.73	0.73	0.0	0.73	0.0	N/A	N/A	N/A	N/A	N/A	N/A
Wayne County											
Number of patches	2025	2026	1.0	2026	1.0	2025	0.0	2025	0.0	N/A	N/A
Forest patch mean area (ha)	66.98	66.95	-0.03	66.95	-0.03	66.98	0.00	66.98	0.00	N/A	N/A
Forest patch median area (ha)	0.54	0.54	0.0	0.54	0.0	0.54	0.0	0.54	0.0	N/A	N/A

Figure 11 illustrates the spatial distribution of the change in the number of forest patches by watershed. The small amount of natural gas development had little effect on the number of forest patches in Lackawanna and Wayne Counties.

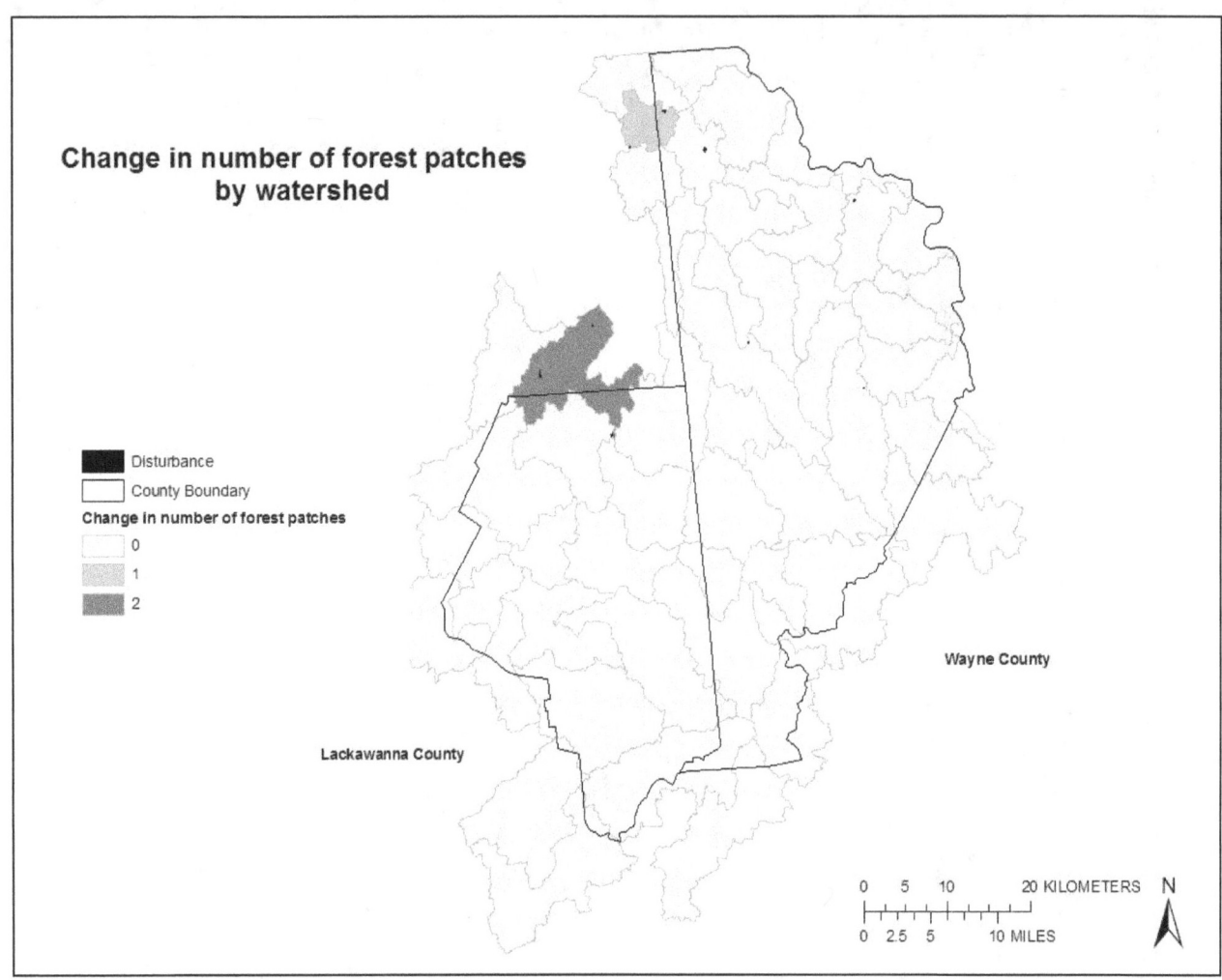

Figure 11. Change in number of forest patches from 2001 to 2010 showing the increasing fragmentation in Lackawanna and Wayne Counties, Pennsylvania. Base-map data courtesy of *The National Map* [(*http://viewer.nationalmap.gov/viewer*) (U.S. Geological Survey, 2011a)].

Interior and Edge Forest

Forest condition (interior and edge) is another way to evaluate the state of the forest. In particular, interior forest is subject to more rapid decline than other segments of the forest. Table 6 shows the change in interior forest and edge forest based on natural gas resource development and the types of natural gas extraction infrastructure. Figures 12 and 13, respectively, illustrate the spatial distribution by watershed of change in percent interior forest and the spatial distribution of change in percent edge forest. The results indicate the following changes occurred based on 2004–2010 natural gas development:

- Neither Lackawanna nor Wayne County showed any forest loss at the county level.

Table 6. Change in percent interior forest and percent edge forest by county for 2001 (original land cover) and as updated for natural gas development disturbance (2004–2010).

[Note: Categories are not mutually exclusive; MS, Marcellus Shale site; non-MS, non-Marcellus Shale site; N/A, Not Applicable—no such infrastructure.]

Metric	Original land cover	Updated with all infra-structure	Change	Updated with MS sites and roads	Change	Updated with non-MS sites and roads	Change	Updated with other infra-structure and roads	Change	Updated with pipelines and roads	Change
Lackawanna County											
Percent forest	62.34	62.34	0.00	62.34	0.00	N/A	N/A	N/A	N/A	N/A	N/A
Percent interior forest	42.36	42.36	0.00	42.36	0.00	N/A	N/A	N/A	N/A	N/A	N/A
Percent Forest edge	14.76	14.76	0.00	14.76	0.00	N/A	N/A	N/A	N/A	N/A	N/A
Wayne County											
Percent forest	71.11	71.11	0.00	71.11	0.00	71.11	0.00	71.11	0.00	N/A	N/A
Percent interior forest	49.90	49.90	0.00	49.90	0.00	49.90	0.00	49.90	0.00	N/A	N/A
Percent forest edge	15.83	15.83	0.00	15.83	0.00	15.83	0.00	15.83	0.00	N/A	N/A

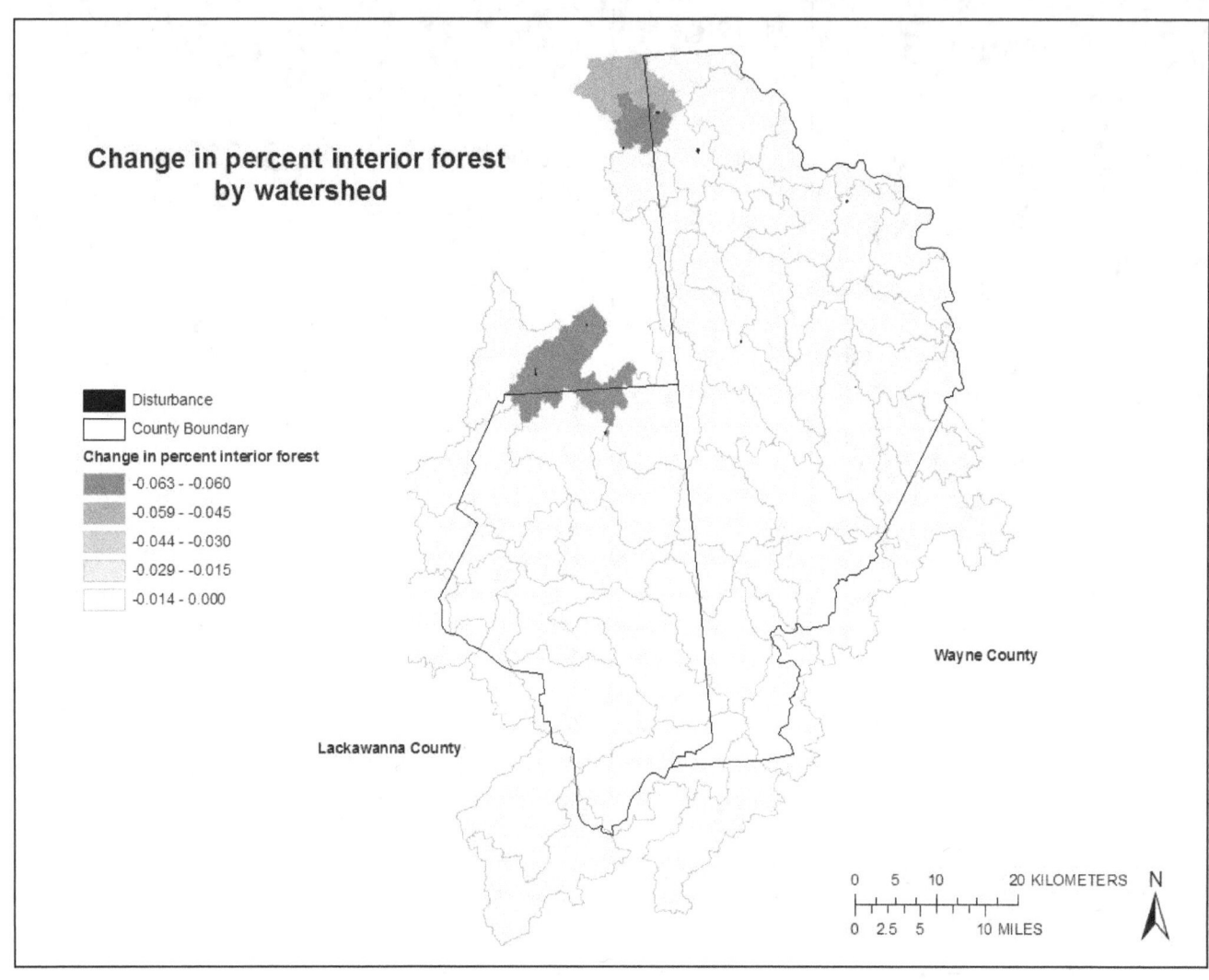

Figure 12. Change in percent interior forest by watershed in Lackawanna and Wayne Counties, Pennsylvania, from 2001 to 2010. Base-map data courtesy of *The National Map* [(*http://viewer.nationalmap.gov/viewer*) (U.S. Geological Survey, 2011a)].

Conclusion

The results presented here show how natural gas extraction in Pennsylvania is affecting the landscape configuration. Neither Lackawanna County nor Wayne County was the location of substantial natural gas development. While the few sites developed were located in forest or on agricultural land, the effects of such development were too small to register with the metrics in use.

The fractal dimension, contagion, and dominance landscape metrics were reported based on recommendations of O'Neill and others (1997); however, these metrics do not appear to be important in these counties. They may be of greater importance for other counties and are reported here for consistency.

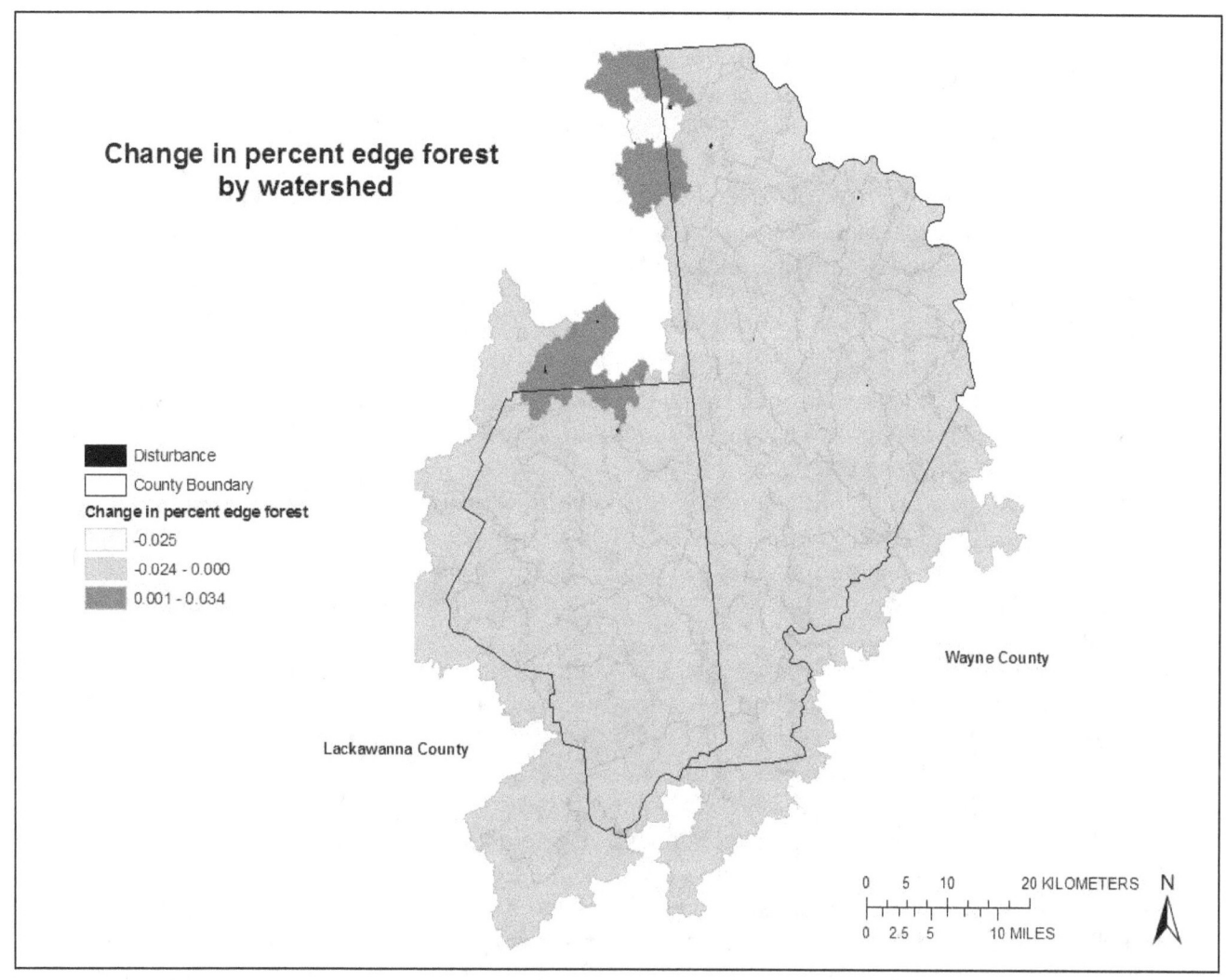

Figure 13. Change in percent of edge forest by watershed in Lackawanna and Wayne Counties, Pennsylvania, from 2001 to 2010. Base-map data courtesy of *The National Map* [(*http://viewer.nationalmap.gov/viewer*) (U.S. Geological Survey, 2011a)].

References Cited

Bonan, G.B., 2008, Forest and climate change; Forcings, feedbacks, and the climate benefits of trees: Science, v. 320, p. 1,444–1,449.

Coleman, J.L., Milici, R.C., Cook, T.A., Charpentier, R.R., Kirschbaum, Mark, Klett, T.R., Pollastro, R.M., and Schenk, C.J., 2011, Assessment of undiscovered oil and gas resources of the Devonian Marcellus Shale of the Appalachian Basin Province, 2011: U.S. Geological Survey Fact Sheet 2011–3092, 2 p., accessed November 17, 2011, at *http://pubs.usgs.gov/fs/2011/3092/*.

Dale, V.H., Brown, Sandra, Haeuber, R.A., Hobbs, N.T., Huntly, N.J., Naiman, R.J., Riesbsame, W.E., Turner, M.G., and Valone, T.J., 2000, Ecological principles and guidelines for managing the use of land: Ecological Society of America report, Ecological Applications, v. 10, no. 3, p. 639–670.

Ebert, D.W., and Wade, T.G., 2004, Analytical tools interface for landscape assessments (ATtILA) user's guide: EPA Report EPA/600/R-04/083, Las Vegas, Nev., accessed October 5, 2011, at *http://epa.gov/esd/land-sci/attila/manual/userman.htm.*

Fahrig, Lenore, and Merriam, Gray, 1994, Conservation of fragmented populations: Conservation Biology, v. 8, no. 1, p. 50–59.

Gardner, Robert, Milne, Bruce, Turner, Monica, and O'Neill, Robert, 1987, Neutral models for the analysis of broad-scale landscape pattern: Landscape Ecology, v. 1, no. 1, p. 19–28.

Gascon, Claude, Williamson, G.B., and da Fonseca, G.A.B., 2007, Receding forest edges and vanishing reserves: Science, v. 288, no. 5470, p. 1,356–1,358.

Gibbs, J.P., and Shriver, W. G., 2005, Can road mortality limit populations of pool-breeding amphibians: Wetlands Ecology and Management, v. 13, p. 281–289.

Gross, D.A., 2005, Ecology III, Inc., Birds; Review of status in Pennsylvania: Pennsylvania Biological Survey, The Ornithological Technical Committee, accessed March 14, 2012, at *http://www.altoona.psu.edu/pabs/bird.html.*

Harper, K.A., MacDonald, S.E., Burton, P.J., Chen, Jiquan, Brosofske, K.D., Saunders, S.C., Euskirchen, E.S., Roberts, Dar, Jaiteh, M.S., and Esseen, Per-Anders, 2005, Edge influence on forest structure and composition in fragmented landscapes: Conservation Biology, v. 19, no. 3, p. 768–782.

Hayden, B.P., 1998, Ecosystem feedbacks on climate at the landscape scale: Philosophical Transactions of the Royal Society B., v. 353, p. 5–18.

Homer, Collin, Dewitz, Jon, Fry, Joyce, Coan, Michael, Hossain, Nazmul, Larson, Charles, Herold, Nate, McKerrow, Alexa, VanDriel, J.N., and Wickham, James, 2007, Completion of the 2001 National Land Cover Database for the conterminous United States: Photogrammetric Engineering and Remote Sensing, v. 73, no. 4, p. 337–341.

Johnson, Nels, 2010, Pennsylvania energy impacts assessment, Report 1: Marcellus Shale Natural Gas and Wind, The Nature Conservancy, Pennsylvania Chapter, and Pennsylvania Audubon,   accessed November13, 2012, at *http://www.nature.org/media/pa/pa_energy_assessment_report.pdf.*

Kuchler, A.W., 1964, Map of potential natural vegetation of the conterminous United States: Special Publication No. 36, New York, American Geographical Society, scale 1:3,168,000.

Laurance, W.F., Nascimento, H.E.M., Laurance, S.G., Andrade, A.C.S., Ewers, R.M., Harms, K.E., Luizao, R.C.C., and Ribeiro, J.E.L.S., 2007, Habitat fragmentation, variable edge effects, and the landscape-divergence hypothesis: PLoS ONE, v. 10, no. 10, p. e1017, doi:10.1371/journal.pone.0001017, accessed October 12, 2011, at *http://www.plosone.org/article/info:doi/10.1371/journal.pone.0001017.*

Lehmkuhl, J.F., and Ruggiero, L.F., 1991, Forest fragmentation in the Pacific Northwest and its potential effects on wildlife, *in* Ruggiero, L.F., Aubry, K.B., Carey, A.B., and Huff, M.H., technical coordinators, Wildlife and vegetation of unmanaged Douglas-fir forests, GTR–PNW–285: U.S. Department of Agriculture, Forest Service, Pacific Northwest Research Station, Portland, Oreg., p. 34–36.

Marzluff, J.M., and Ewing, Kern, 2001, Restoration of fragmented landscapes for the conservation of birds: A general framework and specific recommendations for urbanizing landscapes: Restoration Ecology, v. 9, p. 280–292.

McGarigal, Kevin, Cushman, S.A., Neel, M.C., and Ene, Eduard, 2002, FRAGSTATS: Spatial Pattern Analysis Program for Categorical Maps (computer software program produced by the authors at the University of Massachusetts, Amherst, Mass.), accessed May 31, 2011, at *http://www.umass.edu/landeco/research/fragstats/fragstats.html.*

Nilsson, Greta, 2005, Endangered species handbook: Washington, D.C., Animal Welfare Institute, accessed July 23, 2012, at *http://www.endangeredspecieshandbook.org.*

O'Neill, R.V., Hunsaker, C.T., Jones, K.B., Riitters, K.B., Wickham, J.D., Schwartz, P.M., Goodman, I.A., Jackson, B.L., and Baillargeon, W.S., 1997, Monitoring environmental quality at the landscape scale: BioScience, v. 47, no. 8, p. 513–519.

Pennsylvania Department of Conservation and Natural Resources, 2011, Penns Woods: Pennsylvania Department of Conservation and Natural Resources Web site, accessed March 14, 2012, at *http://www.dcnr.state.pa.us/forestry/pennswoods.aspx.*

Pennsylvania Department of Environmental Protection, 2011, Office of Oil and Gas Management: Pennsylvania Department of Environmental Protection Web site, accessed October 6, 2011, at *http://www.portal.state.pa.us/portal/server.pt/community/oil_and_gas_reports/20297.*

Pennsylvania Parks and Forests Foundation, 2010, History of parks and forests: Pennsylvania Parks and Forests Foundation Web site, accessed March 14, 2012, at *http://www.paparksandforests.org/history.html.*

Riitters, K.H., O'Neill, R.V., Hunsaker, C.T., Wickham, J.D., Yankee, D.H., Timmins, S.P., Jones, K.B., and Jackson, B.L., 1995, A factor analysis of landscape pattern and structure metrics: Landscape Ecology, v. 10, no. 1, p. 23–39.

Riitters, K.H., O'Neill, R.V., Wickham, J.D., and Jones, K.B., 1996, A note on contagion indices for landscape analysis: Landscape Ecology, v. 11, no. 4, p. 197–202.

Riitters, K.H, Wickham, J.D., O'Neill, R.V., Jones, K.B., and Smith, E.R., 2000, Global-scale patterns of forest fragmentation: Conservation Ecology, v. 4, no. 2, accessed July 12, 2012, at *http://www.consecol.org/vol4/iss2/art3/.*

Skole, D.L., and Tucker, C.J., 1993, Tropical deforestation and habitat fragmentation in the Amazon; Satellite data from 1978 to 1988: Science, v. 260, no. 5116, p. 1,905–1,910.

Slonecker, Terrence, Milheim, Lesley, and Claggett, Peter, 2010, Landscape indicators and land cover change in the Mid-Atlantic region of the United States, 1973–2001: GIScience and Remote Sensing, v. 47, no. 2, p. 163–186.

Stevens, S.H., and Kuuskraa, V.A., 2009, Gas shale—1: Seven plays dominate North America activity: Oil & Gas Journal, Special Report: Trends in Unconventional Gas, v. 107, no. 36, p. 39–49, accessed April 9, 2012, at *http://www.ogj.com/articles/print/volume-107/issue-36/Drilling___Production/special-report-gas-shale-1-seven-plays-dominate-north-america-activity.html.*

Turner, M.G., 2005, Landscape ecology; What is the state of the science?: Annual Reviews Ecology and Evolutionary Systems, v. 36, p. 319–344.

Turner, M.G., Gardner, R.H., and O'Neill, R.V., 2001, Landscape ecology in theory and practice: New York, Springer-Verlag, 401 p.

U.S. Department of Agriculture, Farm Service Agency, 2011, Aerial Photography Field Office: U.S. Department of Agriculture Web page, accessed October 26, 2011, at *http://www.fsa.usda.gov/FSA/apfoapp?area=home&subject=prog&topic=nai.*

U.S. Department of Agriculture, Natural Resources Conservation Service, 2011, Geospatial Data Gateway: U.S. Department of Agriculture Web page, accessed August 26, 2011, at *http://datagateway.nrcs.usda.gov/.*

U.S. Geological Survey, 2011a, *The National Map*: U.S. Geological Survey National Map home page, accessed October 17, 2011, at *http://nationalmap.gov/.*

U.S. Geological Survey, 2011b, National Hydrography Dataset: U.S. Geological Survey National Dataset home page, accessed April 6, 2012, at *http://nhd.usgs.gov/data.html.*

U.S. Geological Survey, 2011c, National Land Cover Database (NLCD): U.S. Geological Survey database, accessed June 1, 2011, at *http://www.mrlc.gov/finddata.php*.

U.S. Geological Survey, 2012, Energy Resources Program: U.S. Geological Survey Web site, accessed July 6, 2012, at *http://energy.usgs.gov/Tools/EnergyDataFinderSplash.aspx*.

West Virginia Geological and Economic Survey, 2011, Selected references about Devonian shales: West Virginia Geological and Economic Survey Web page, accessed November 17, 2011, at *http://www.wvgs.wvnet.edu/www/datastat/devshales.htm*.

White, P.S., and Pickett, S.T.A., 1985, Natural disturbance and patch dynamics; An introduction, *in* Pickett, S.T.A., and White, P.S., eds., The ecology of natural disturbance and patch dynamics: Orlando, Fla., Academic Press, p. 3–9.

Wickham, J.D., O'Neill, R.V., Riitters, K.H., Wade, T.G., and Jones, K.B., 1997, Sensitivity of selected landscape pattern metrics to land-cover misclassification and differences in land-cover composition: Photogrammetric Engineering & Remote Sensing, v. 63, no. 4, p. 397–402.

Wickham, J.D., and Riitters, K.H., 1995, Sensitivity of landscape metrics to pixel size: International Journal of Remote Sensing, v. 16, no. 18, p. 3,585–3,594.

Wickham, J.D., Riitters, K.H., Wade, T.G., Coan, Michael, and Homer, Collin, 2007, The effect of Appalachian mountaintop mining on interior forest: Landscape Ecology, v. 22, p. 179–187.

Wickham, J.D., Wade, T.G., and Riitters, K.H., 2008, Detecting temporal change in watershed nutrient yields: Environmental Management, v. 42, p. 223–231.

With, K.A., and Pavuk, D.M., 2011, Habitat area trumps fragmentation effects on arthropods in an experimental landscape system: Landscape Ecology, v. 26, p. 1,035–1,048.